on Hysteria

on Hysteria

NANCY KUHL

Published in the United Kingdom in 2022 by Shearsman Books Ltd
PO Box 4239
SWINDON
SN3 9FN
www.shearsman.com

Shearsman Books Ltd Registered Office
30-31 St. James Place, Mangotsfield, Bristol BS16 9JB
(this address is not for correspondence)

ISBN 978-1-84861-837-4

Complete citations for works referenced in *On Hysteria* can be found online: www.phylumpress.com/on-hysteria-notes.

DESIGN Megan Mangum, Words That Work

Acknowledgements

Sincere thanks to the editors of *Conjunctions Online*, *HERE*, *The Nation*, *SplitLevel*, and *Tab* in which some of these poems originally appeared; to the curators of *Crevice Communities* at Charles Sturt University for including "Rock and Rook" in that exhibition; and to the editors of A Published Event who included several of these poems in their Lost Rocks series with the title *Granite*.

I am grateful to Jane Tillman, Lee Watroba, and their colleagues at the Erikson Institute, Stockbridge, MA, for my extraordinary experience as an Erikson Scholar in Residence in 2016.

This work benefited enormously from my course of study as a Research Fellow at the Western New England Institute for Psychoanalysis, New Haven, CT; many thanks to friends and colleagues there.

And deep thanks, as ever, to dearest friends and collaborators: Jen Bervin, Anne Dailey, Richard Deming, Karla Kelsey, Anna Leahy, Megan Mangum, Caitlin Mitchell, Justy Phillips, Karin Roffman, Elizabeth Willis, Margaret Woodward, and Timothy G. Young.

Dear Stranger

Some poems herein refer to or borrow language from *Studies on Hysteria*, by Josef Breuer and Sigmund Freud, 1895; and *A Fragment of an Analysis of a Case of Hysteria*, by Sigmund Freud, 1905. Specific references are to *The Standard Edition of the Complete Psychological Works of Sigmund Freud*, translated by James Strachey.

Table of Contents

I. Hysteria Gloss

II. A Turn in the Plot

III. Tidal Reach

Hysterics suffer mainly from reminiscences.
— Sigmund Freud, *Studies on Hysteria*, 1895

Critics of the family were called hysterics.
— Adam Phillips, *Becoming Freud*, 2014

I. Hysteria Gloss

One Story House

The indifferent backdoor propped open.
Somewhere nearby tides empty the river,

fill it: honest pressures of the moon.
In a family, when something has been lost

something new can be recruited to take its place.
The threshold, it almost demands action: look

toward the world, its temporary quality
of wholeness, or else the parts into which

it is divided. The frame it makes, that door,
year by year; a structure for seeing, a gap

in the curtain: stage and actors, the astonished
audience. In a family, the way sides are chosen:

if we were talking about the migration of birds,
we'd say *the influence of the wind*.

Hysteria Gloss

When a good or a bad trait is absent say
it skips a generation;

ache or blurt or blear: a symptom
confirms our suspicions;

of reluctance say
she can't pull the trigger;

a gasping distinction shimmering
in river mud: the rumors are true;

diagnosis: she has a tendency to disappear
suddenly and without warning;

enduring long periods of uncertainty,
anyone might become a scavenger.

Accounts

When I began to tell it, you said: *try to*
make something sensible rather than
something beautiful. One of us has gotten
it all wrong.

                    Burnt tongue or bee sting:
a minor wound might be at the center
(forgotten, consequential: who knows now
which blurry instant, the exact damage?).

Then moonlight with its grim
suspicions.

                    When I couldn't hold it
in my mind, the story took shape in my lungs.

—

A common literary theme: *difficult*
circumstances can be changed. Remember

Man's inhumanity to man? That is:
sometimes c*ircumstances* means *a man*,

not *difficult* so much as *vicious* or *lethal*
and *changed* means *one of us has to go*

or *no one is safe.* Sometimes in a novel
a rising moon marks a revelation, a turn

in the plot. In the real world, in your actual
life, has moonlight ever changed anything?

—

A father spends years perfecting
his hatred. One daughter is a double

agent: undercover or going to ground.
One records everything in the margins

of paperback novels. Summer holidays,
they strolled the boardwalk like any family

(nobody says anything – this distinguishes
them from the families in books).

This family, this suburban dead-end
family—they use silence like a rope.

—

It's nothing special; anything
knitted is made of knots.

Shadow
falling: a fraction, a trace, a figure's
recognizable shape. That's *sequence*;
try to name *function*.

If her life were
like a magic show, what would be

the trapdoor opening to the grimy
crawlspace beneath the stage?

A magician tips his hat. Someone's
daughter turns into a bird.

—

Gathering clouds and the moon
slides out of view. The clouds

slide, I mean. Wind comes up
out of nowhere. Pushed beyond

the frame; vagrant rather
than vanished. Distraction, then,

and delay. Find graphite focus.
Soon it's so far and high;

it's become so slight I might blow it
aside like dust from my eraser.

—

The voice of the present tense begins
to waver, trail off. The story is a crick

in the neck; the bones becoming
soft, accepting the impression

of touch.

By *story*, I mean *the given*
account or *what was told*. Bones are

bones; they don't stand in for *resolve*
or *enterprise* or *imagination*.
The same

moon drags the sea back and forth again.
Even this might become a new idea.

See Through

Tarnished dull the mirror; crack
and feather kiss cheek and brow.

Sun-sheer dress, summer's
last afternoon. How it carries on,

the old secret, suspended
in brackish air, air too heavy

to fill the lungs. Enduring.
Like the ancient glass marked

with fleck and mottle. Then—
her silver likeness. Long forsaken

the mirror: the edges, now light moves
straight through. Shrug or shudder.

Blink the mind blank. Place blame
like a row of stitches at the hem.

Hysteria

Skin translucent, veins divide blue to blue: the convenient comfort of fingers hiding eyes makes vision changeable. Untrustworthy. Knows no mind, the body. In cavernous happenstance, in uncertain dusk, in danger—the moment slips out of control. We require some subsequent, some consequently. Blame the physiology of equilibrium, that merciless truth: in the half-life of hand to wrist, that spectral longing, the clever body glows, refuses to comply. All you have to do is touch me. Meanwhile, we hold the chair's broken back accountable for our daily treachery, for breath in splinters. No matter what you wish for or how you want it: body body body, dumb and madly insubordinate. Meanwhile we softly, we signify, we linger like the blood that rings the nail bed. Unmistakable, the pattern can catch us by surprise; we burn our impressions into beams, into brick. We have no other choice. This is the memory of events witnessed while sleepwalking. This is a language of tip and spill (every utterance means *carefully*). And when I think I'll suffocate? This is the necessary breath. We have no other.

see "... the connection is not so simple. It consists only in what might be called a 'symbolic' relation between the precipitating cause and the pathological phenomena—a relation such as healthy people form in dreams." On the Psychical Mechanism of Hysterical Phenomena.

Cul-de-Sac

I

Hidden thicket hollow,
forest in sheltered sliver:

alone in the wildest corner
of the yard. And nearby

the human interior, raised
upstairs voices emptied

of specific meaning.
Sound (or something inside

the syllables) uncoiling, slack
and slippery as silk ribbon.

2

On a bicycle, a child circles:
exquisite summer boredom. I could

say: *maybe you have a lucky stone*
in your pocket or an unlucky stone

in your shoe. When she stops and
shields her eyes with her hand, I

could say: *what comes next is less*
like this clear gesture than it is

like the distance between us.
                                        In my mind
I say aloud: *what do you see?*

Archival Footage

Fingers square a frame, shape
the camera's demands.

View: girl gazing to green
middle distance, to far off

concrete-seamed lot. Cut then
to her magnificent friends,

untouchable adolescent promise
glowing, waiting together

on the platform when off-screen
a voice shouts *Run*. The camera—

its reliable vision reels then:
spectacular panic of suburban

landscape. Sudden patch of blue
so bright it makes our mouths water.

A Case History

Firelight and something
impossible—scuttle and dash—

just out of sight. Then her arms
fall asleep (*pins-and-needles* or

make-believe). How like a statue
she becomes, stone tribute to mis-

placed history: every ancient moment—
time and time and time—present

and available and gathered into her
senseless limbs (gathered like petal

and stem and thorn). Distant, the sun
sinks. Later, it will rise. The rose

garden fountain spills the same water
all season, all over. Finally, when

she opens her still-sweet mouth it is
full of papery scales, of cinder

and ash. Or it is full of a foreign
tongue—words she almost sings.

see "The course of the illness fell into several clearly separable phases..."
Case I: Fräulein Anna O.

Ghost Story

The last family lived
here (it seemed true)

for a hundred years. We
inherit cracked tiles and

blistering plaster and pieces
of broken, bewildering

things. Another girl
slept behind this door;

smudged prints—her whole
fingers—grip the sill.

A spine-broken ghost story says:
see-through girl, empty as a cello.

Is that: lost-to-this-world, she's
a wide-open chamber of vibration,

the very foundation of song?
Or, like in the house at the end

of the street, she is electric crackle
orange-hot, sparks from the socket.

Always we've known it:
she's not going anywhere.

Inground Pool

Persistent, suburbia's
concrete wish: to forget

gradual boundaries
and descending banks;

to ignore unpredictable
margins, that moving

line where water naturally
encounters ground.

The Drawing of Granite Bay

We search for what will hold
it all together: solid ground-
work or speed steadily increasing.

We pretend it's a faraway shoreline
but from any hill you see sky-
scrapers standing in toothy rows.

Ice will break, eventually, the crust
and also hidden structures (structures
that tell us nothing about bone).

There isn't anything so old as this.

—

A child eating brilliant pink
flowers (lips and teeth frame
slender, pointy petals);

                                        an actress
sinking in quicksand in a black-and-
white-matinee jungle.

                                        Ancient middle-
class ambition, the blades of greener
grass. She undecorates the basic concept.

She becomes an escape artist,
slips through any kind of grasp.

She's as good as gone.

—

The surface of the ocean
isn't still but there's no

disturbance. Pencil
marks the terrain's

curving, tracing the path
to the margin, sun-bleached

or silted under. Vertical
cliff and rising cedar. Paper

unfurls, blues streaming.
The map, the mind's eye.

—

Now what? or *What were you*
thinking? Rumor drifting

to the surface, then; through
sediment and swell to the sunlit

and rippled. And *What does*
any of it have to do with me?

Soon, it would be told, but what
was broken was still breaking.

Who do you think you are? then.
And later: *What have I done?*

—

It was a troubled summer, a period
of powerful thirst. And then some-

one broke a window and climbed in.
What I lost: all the jewelry I ever

owned (except the silver bracelet
on my wrist). And my grandfather's

initials engraved on the back
of a watch. That was late October.

Leaning into frost. And then a mild
winter. And then a cold spring.

—

The purpose was to record it:
hollows and stony tracks and

the road's surprising and decisive
bend. To get it all down. On paper,

over gridded lines. How does a map
become a record of waiting? Of not

wanting? Bank, estuary, swamp:
plotted. American lawns, driveways.

Hours stretch taut, unbending.
What will survive our forgetfulness?

Footnote (A Case History)

I said I
was quite

convinced
something

else had
happened

and she gave
way then,

she let fall
a single phrase;

she'd hardly
said a word

before her
old father—

he was still
sitting there

behind her—
before her

father began
to sob bitterly.

see "Naturally I pressed my investigation no further..."
Case 2: Frau Emmy von N.

Wrecked

On black ice she accelerates into
swerve and *heave*—she can't help it.

She thinks: *wrecked*, as if the car
has crashed already or a meteor;

as if a sledgehammer or a fury.
Or a family's desperate striving

resolved into pennilessness.
There's relief in the tires' eventual

glide. She considers the gift, the pale
dress; she considers her unyielding

spine, her pair of working lungs,
her attentive nerve endings.

Pleats in rows like rib and rib.
Greedy grip on elbow or wrist.

What fastens her to this or any night
is thin and pliant: silver thread, stitch

and suture. Spinning now she's given up
all sense of where it begins. She's beyond

every kind of appraisal. Hips, shoulder blades—
whose is it, her singular and common body?

Look: the car's predictable progress,
it's so much slower than you'd imagine.

II. A Turn in the Plot

Complaints of Profound Darkness

Behind a scrim or visible in outline;
drunken or broken or struck—

struck, as if by force.

—

A life has surface tension and
yet it can break: she is on a spot-
lit stage, or on a weary staircase

when layers blur or a glorious haze
blooms or she enters a blackness
absolute and awake with reason.

—

A shell that fails to fire; a bet before
the cards are dealt; a place to hide.

—

First her language dropped
the marks of steady time.

Names tumbled then and
objects; words seemed

suddenly to describe
nothing at all. Next and

swiftly she covered
her mouth. And then

and then and then she
quit speaking altogether.

—

A penny on the
thin skin of each lid.

—

As a worm as a beetle as a bat as a mole as a stone.

—

Lacking discernment
or insight; having

no eyes. Blind.
As in *stunned*.

—

Glare and mirror and seeing
double a sparrow hits the glass;
breaks its neck striking flawless

reflection. In sight of such clear
confusion, any girl's heart
might, momentarily, seem to stop.

see "At moments when her mind was quite clear she would complain of the profound darkness in her head, of not being able to think, of becoming blind and deaf, of having two selves, a real one and an evil one which forced her to behave badly, and so on." Case 1: Fräulein Anna O.

Along the Grain

We say *sleep like a stone*;
we mean *like the dead.*

In the time of nightmares, this
is wishful thinking. In the time

of sleepwalking. No one—not even
our sleeper—can say what happens

in these rooms after midnight.
In the dreams the sea is as haunted

as the house; it's dull and red,
no horizon, no end in sight.

—

We worried about the trains.
We tried to remember to wind

the clock in the hall (*Grandfather
Clock* is only a song; mine stood

behind a hardware store counter;
was more *wristwatch* than w*eight-

driven plumb*). You might say we
lingered in expectation. Longing

which suggests sadness; not *wanting*
with its implication of deficiency.

—

What little we were able to say.
The question was finally asked:

names and dates, verb, verb—gush
and spill. Abrupt new honesty

puts an end to thinking.
I wanted
wait tell me again tell me more.

I dreamt of water rising through
the dirt, through the floorboards;

I dreamt of the staircase climbing
into a fire on the second floor.

—

The smooth or pebbled, the hot,
the solid, the immovable. Unknow-

able interior. There is no floor plan
or frame. No method. Liquid hardening

in seamed layers. Something like
the creased-soft postcard (long ago,

faraway) but also like the crack-
veined hand mirror (reflection, shatter).

This is what happens. This is what
happens. This is what happens.

—

Sameness of daily routine; ordinary
disruptions. Afternoon train

sounding over the bridge. Chime
and tick and the clock is wound

again, slows again. Someone calls
children home at dusk. Their names.

Stillness follows. The atmosphere—
it can break into pieces across

the high-fenced yard. Night comes
down finally, closing like an eye.

—

By morning, I've forgotten,
mostly, though I remember

my father was there
(wherever we were)

(whoever *we* were).
And I woke crying out

again. I woke saying, as I am
always saying in the dreams

that wake me this way,
I was saying (trying to say) *no.*

The Talking Cure

1

To be alive now
is to take this

into consideration:
the bottom of breath

is nearly not human.
Turn sound toward

meaning by force.
Mouthful of gravel

or moss and
language,

this language—
bloodied, in pieces.

Monstrous,
misshapen thing.

2

Worn out and
nerve-shot,

her ache is ramble
then rant. Or

it's a language
half heard,

halfhearted.
Her pain is a voice

pulled by handfuls
from the throat.

see "... and finally her disturbances of speech were 'talked away'..."
Case 1: Fräulein Anna O.

Half Sisters Story

Absent from every shining and
every withered memory, chain-link

backyard afternoons and starlit sailboat
rockings. Nobody's daughter; sister like

something I slept through. The too-late
awareness that she had meant nothing—

it strikes at the horizon like heat lightning.
How is it she arrives without disrupting

the silence? My muscle-deep longing
to take flight—is this regret? Is it hunger?

A Case History

The warp of it, her sight, is a memorial
to some ephemeral revelation, an instant—

sudden and vivid and obvious—the background
coming into focus. Mindless and without,

in a split-open second of flash and tweak:
she authors a bright new smallness.

At once, everything adapts to her method
of blur and diminish. She laces the family

together (they whisper and coax and wish).
It's easy now to find oneself lost in thought.

She was taken in by their complete and brutal
love. Until that moment, holding still

as for a camera. Until, in that golden dazzlement,
she saw the world and the world saw her.

see "We shall be reminded, moreover, of hysterical macropsia..."
Case 2: Frau Emmy von N.

Archival Footage

Bubbled and tape-
spliced, lost-and-

found film flickers
to focus: anonymous

ancestor strolling
a garden stoops

to break a stem.
When and then

sun catches her
jeweled pin, glint

momentarily strikes
the lens, flashes

ahead and finds me
now, watching.

Preserved and living,
our long-silent-

instant, this private
theater, this unspooling.

Her decades and
mine. There are

days and days
to come and nights.

This History in Fragments Called Stone

Two turn into a third;
each and
both. So like themselves.

Matrix (I am easily bewildered
by the language).
And: lazurite,

calcite, sodalite. Under. Sub sub-
terranean lapis pressing not-yet-

blues to crack and pucker. Eventually:
ultramarine.
Joints knuckle.

Stone polished and aglow:
an undiscovered planet.

—

As in a fable: we thought we'd move
to remote woods, a tiny cabin (this,
when we knew we were truly and

at last alone). But the dapple and chill,
that nearly perfect not-quiet. Just
the thought—well, it dragged us low.

We live now under high ceilings
on a rocky coast; youthful trees offer
inviting shade.

We devote one hour
each afternoon to ordinary unhappiness.

—

A crisis, another. Pressure heats
everything. Slowly at first, then
rushing. Little by little and then
all at once.
The situation is quite
serious; it's dire; maybe you should
come; you should come.
Picture
a scrim. No—picture a sentence
struck through: intrusion of ink.
Letter forms remain; almost remain.
Meaning comes gradually apart.

—

Try thinking through a mineral lens.
Now stillness is method, progression

by inactivity. Grit and grain under
palm, surface hot under late sun.

Depressions collect rain, ponding, pooling.
Airy mosses—nearly invisible stem and

flower—reach into seams with roots
unrecognizable as roots.

Cold comes crisp and influencing.
It cracks the whole earth open wide.

—

What comes up through layers.
The top, the lip, the overlay,
the brink, the joint, the skim,
the skin.
                    What happens happens
by minutes and by hours—it's true
here and anywhere.
                                        One then
the next. This then this
then this. And and and.
                                        Soon
we'll say the structure loses
its regular form; becomes a jumble.

—

One story is time beyond
comprehension. The end.

There is something called
a melt; it has a plot: beginning,

middle, and *the last of it*.
And the fever when it forms.

Solid parentrock and
percolation along margins.

And see how it takes a shine.
The end, the end, the end.

see "...you will be able to convince yourself that much will be gained if we succeed in transforming your hysterical misery into common unhappiness." The Psychotherapy of Hysteria.

Feral

Longing distorts its object and soon
(like a child going hungry all afternoon)

she stops the beating in her chest (moves it
instead for a while into her skull). This

condition persists beyond pang and craving
(loops endless, clock-hands-turning).

Once she lived among others; now
she's gone feral. That word, vibrating,

is a hunch. A dawning. It arrives like birds
returning to the window ledge, familiar

and violent (the truth about starlings).
She aims for the space between mouth

and sound—*syllable, syllable.* Panting,
creaturely. Her voice confirms it:

thought direct as touching. Nevertheless—
from the doorway, who wouldn't admire

her sunlit room, the wing-beaten
episode outside the window? And

the glass between them, solid and
brittle, transparent and impossibly blue?

Rock and Root

1 *Field Guide*

Stem and leaf in spare drawings—
nothing like stem and leaf. About

moss: *sea moss is not a moss;*
reindeer moss is not a moss.

Goes on like this for three pages.
The lesson might be: *what you think*

you know is wrong. On stone what
grows grows like paint or polish,

like a spill spreading across a table.
I study the drawings; I'm easily fooled.

2 *Postcard*

Not *climbed* – we drifted.
Do you remember? To

the smoothest ledge (air
too shallow for breathing).

That rock, how it held us;
how it suspended the inevitable

rest of the day. We talked
and talked; we each lied a little

(but only that much). I've all but
forgotten every word we said.

3 *Field Guide*

Of lichens, at first the message
seems so much the same: *lichens are
like plants, but they are not plants.*

Then, the improbable shift: *they can
seem to live on thin air.* And: *anchored
by a holdfast, lichen can grow
inside solid rock, between the grains.*

Holdfast. My skin is prickle and itch.
Confounding, the absolute intimacy
of this earthly accomplishment.

4 *Tested a Theory*

I remembered you there. No.
Not you there. I mean: *in that forest,*

I thought of you. Riven shelf above
the lake, end of the trail – we didn't

stop to think. We jumped. I mean:
with others, I swam – you weren't there.

If it's an argument, we're still in it.
This, an idea in a body in icy water

(sundrenched and breathless and
floating; newly deliberate).

5 *Observation and Identification*

Like a needle, like a river,
like antlers, like fingers, like

threads.
Consider other subtle
distinctions – *grip* and *catch*

versus *hold* and *fasten*. How
uncertainties inherent in difference

recall mistakes occasioned
by similarity.
Bent like a sickle,

keeled like a boat; tongue-shaped;
jagged, sharp – like a row of teeth.

6 *Dear Reader*

Now it's winter where we climbed;
where rock and root; where break and
sun and lake and lichen and moss.

There's
no sure language at this elevation;
wind carves a path of howl and echo.

Cleave contradicts itself: *to split*
apart by force of a cutting blow;
and *to attach and hold fast.*
Then,
too, *fast* sometimes means *to move*
swiftly.
Confusion can also be a certainty.

Landline

Season of howl and
hiss, season of

my stubborn falter.
I attend midnight

pines keening, alive
with some haunting,

with talons, with
wings. I wake

almost without
having slept;

you call, you
invent listening again.

The Windy Planet

We live surrounded now by saltwater.

—

Songbirds sing night into scaffolding built by trees.

—

Regardless, we can't forget the old brick walls,
the ruse. We collaborate on chronology,
just what was said; we keep whispering
about triangles and whim; we go on
seeking a true version: *what happened.*

—

Saltwater makes weather or
we do or the birds do.

—

After a season—we've barely unpacked—
this becomes the windy planet. Relentless
storms; trees crash down after upright centuries.

—

It can seem possible to sleep through
any catastrophe.
                                        Saltwater rolls and
waves. It carries us. We are carried.

III. Tidal Reach

Analogies

I

annotations in the margin
building of several stories
buried city
crystallization
disloyal sisters
double flowers
electric lighting system
falling from the sky
festoons of flowers twined around a wire
ghosts in the underworld
house with many windows
Knight's move
opera prince disguised as beggar
pearl in oyster
pictographic script (in that alphabet *being sick* means
disgust)
pine-shavings for kindling wood
rock and root
serial story
sounding-board and tuning-fork
strangers share a secret
stratified structure
superimposition
theft of something priceless
telephone wire
three wishes
unlocking a door

2

an unnavigable river
whose stream is
at one moment choked
by masses of rock
and at another
divided and lost
among shallows
and sandbanks

see General Indexes; *also* "Breuer and I had often compared the symptomatology of hysteria..." Case 4: Katharina; ***and*** "This first account..." Case fragment: Dora.

Threshold

1 *Wildflowers*

When it suddenly seemed too much
to contemplate, you said: *divide*
the idea into parts.
My vulnerability
is new and unprecedented; I am
fragile in all the same old ways.

Today: opened like wildflowers; like
wildflowers bent against rain. Red
petals, the smallest increments;
I ask for help
again. There's more talking; each word
an artifact of something already lost.

2 *To Swift*

To try to formulate an answer. To think
only of running; to wait. To feel hunger begin,

as it sometimes does, in the fingertips. To
recall last year and last week as if moving

across a threshold. To pry open the romance,
hold it open. To slowly grow smaller (curl in-

ward, fern-like). To find a letter behind the desk;
to consider, in this way, a gap between *missing*

and *lost.* To write or to say it. Half gone. To swift;
to wait. To turn past the sound of your voice.

3 *Meteor*

Ice and rock rushing now. Falling.
Burning sphere, as predicted. Promised.

Clarity, velocity. And the force with which
you respond (I mean *say nothing*).

Unconditional plummet, an absolute
fact; gravity, the thought of it leaves

the weight of salt on the tongue. And
the eye, into which a thousand frozen years

and any hour's sway and proof; the eye,
into which the bright, the dark world rushes.

4 *Eclipse*

Almost any word you'd say about travel
might also be said about time. We have

walked and walked and now we stand
in the shadow of the tree (we say *shade*).

There are words to describe a journey
when it's long and difficult. *Shade* also

means *ghost*. *Eclipse* doesn't only
describe a relationship between

two celestial bodies. Don't forget:
I'm still talking about what light can do.

5 *A Story about Feathers*

100-year-old bodies of shorebirds
contain mineral knowledge (sodium,

sulfur, zinc); compound, crystal,
traces of temporal events—*ocean-*

floor volcano then coastal flood—
recorded in pin and down. Time

writes itself indelible into feather,
into hollow bone. And the past

rises like the sea.
When did
all my ideas become this idea?

6 *A Story about Shadows*

In this room wishes are windows—
ordinary and transparent. Blinds

and branches pattern slant-
wise and shifting (be patient:

trust reliable variation).
Ceiling as field and support,

look up: summer from
the bottom of a green lake.

In this room memory can be a tool or
an instrument (a chisel or a compass).

Family Album

Cracked emulsion, blistered narrative. Family like something seen underwater: vague and metallic and meager. Still they look like us (or might: we study faces, we cast fountain pennies). A family at a table in a curtained kitchen, each face turned in the direction of the camera. New car, chain link fence, dog in the yard. Next, it's winter-gray and every hand is pocketed. In this way, meaning accrues like money—unpredictably over years (*savings* or *deficit* or *debt*). The family may seem to include only those present on a given day; or else, all the long past and forgotten (but here in the palm). Then, too, there is what we cannot afford to lose. Irrevocable, time opens or stands away or breaks into all the frozen colors of ice. These familiar these strange bodies, paper-soft and framed now in every kind of light—the ache in the lungs is undeniably ours, alone.

A Case History

A girl and her teeth.
Awake after all

the others. Sight-
lines, room to room.

Threadbare, wood
worn to splinter,

the house. Faraway
generations, animated

by draught and creak.
A girl and her ribcage.

Time yields, surrenders
yesterday into yesterday.

The girl, she is not dead—
even here, where tired gesture

hones threat and promise.
Even in this rasp and

clench, a century of hearts
beating themselves silent.

A girl and her lungs.
Breathtaken, the house.

see " ...she was choosing shortness of breath ..." Case 4: Katharina.

Cul-de-sac

Like the cement block basement foundation holding the house up as gravity pulls it down: the whole precarious thing threatens to sink. About the house, let's be honest—it is sinking: mud and rock displacing mud and rock. By inch, by year. Once the answer to doubt or disbelief was *see for yourself.* But I keep thinking about the eye—how it loves novelty, how it grows so easily bored. And the tricks it can play. Say I lean against a wall, shoulders flat, palms flat. Me and the wall—we do not hold each other up. Or maybe it's like losing your page in a book: you hunt the hinge dividing what you already know from what's coming next. We say: *find your place.* I want a language that allows and undoes at once. I have such a language. I may as well have said: *I want a language.* From the kitchen window, I watch suburban vultures lean into air, lean into nothing at all. And if it falls to rubble? Not slowly, but all at once: catastrophic clamor and dust curling on currents, certainty rippling around us like a desert mirage. I should have said *when it falls.* For now, I am earthbound; by phenomenon, by force. Or *when it fell.* Dusk and the wordless neighborhood. Heavy forms gathered in pines at the end of the street. Sometimes it can seem like we have no choice but to run.

Elegy

Cut an apple and
ate slices off the blade;

together ankle-deep
the undertow heaving;

language permits the possibility:
it will have been like this.

For you I gave up dreaming
(not for you but to forget you);

familiar shape, shadow
in the hall—your living body.

I shrug my shoulders
when I hear your name.

The Roof

I sleep on the roof (watch
the pitch). The view is treetops,

streetlights, neighbors' gables—
in glimpse and gap and edge.

I am often caught up in reflection
(think: *rewriting every chapter*

from the start not: *the backward*
silvered world spun round).

I sleep well enough to want
to say of the roof *it rocks me.*

Tidal Reach

I

Moving, the river changes
everything—lash and

churn, swallows roots,
trunks of bank-side trees,

their low, flung-wide limbs.
All unsteady; all gone under.

Sky open to the hinge.
Blackmud, bonechill.

Water rises (again
this rushing past).

Find the ancient, the well-
made house, throw every

switch. Flood the rooms
with unremarkable light.

2

Clouds crowd afternoon's edges.
Same old tide rushes in, simplest

measure. I know drowning
isn't a love story still I think

how the swimmer, exhausted,
might drift, finally, drift under;

how current is an embrace. Under-
water any familiar thing might be warped

or swollen, broken or made bright.
It's all I can do not to fall to my knees.

Archival Footage

Someone knew once
but we've forgotten

who and on what
street, which now-

emptied town.
Brittle-film bodies

waver or coalesce
into shuddering

tree rings, some
record of what we've

weathered. You call and
I pick up the phone,

I answer; you say
my name, say *it's me.*

Hysteria

The rigid inside of the wrist, the exact origin of utterance. Take nothing for granted. Air entering, foundation, the shape of it: syllables illustrate meaning. Words the tongue longs for. Day and night I handle ideas and objects (deny myself this, allow myself this). Predictable grammar of inadequacy: I see my shadow fall on the front steps and think *all you have to do is touch me.* The very thing, dear brilliant, dear stranger, the answer: marks on my arm where the dog's teeth sunk in. The story I've been trying to tell you ends like this: when she was momentarily blinded and could not recognize him, he offered her his hands. After all, the body knows something.

see "But she would never begin to talk until she had satisfied herself of my identity by carefully feeling my hands." Case 1: Fräulein Anna O.

Takes Place

Summer rental, buckled pavement
path to a screened porch; every day

we stand at river's edge, watch
the action of currents. We suspect

something; we do not say it aloud.
From the third floor, we are almost

eye-level with stars. Evenings are
gravity and copper and magnetism.

These nouns have no opposites; we
identify others that likewise stand alone.

—

Occasionally we drove
to the beach to swim.

We ignored warnings
about riptides, walked

deliberately into waves.
We know there's no

match for the undertow,
that mindless drag

and pull. No match for
hunger so relentless.

—

The list we made was not unlike
a navigational chart but neither
did it explicitly describe the means.
This is one way of moving into
moving through experience.
Careening as in lurching. I think:
is this how we are meant to know
our minds? What multiplies and
what cancels? With speed and
changeability: reeling and gone.

—

Of each and everything we ask:
what is it like? We describe

the horizon set down between
limit and limitlessness. We

telescope the view through a grid
of screen: narrow harbor,

narrow breakwater. Inevitably,
the mouth of the bay. Some-

one will say something pretty: *It was
all suspended under birds' wings.*

—

Careening is also grounding
a sailboat at low tide, exposing
what is otherwise underwater.

To make necessary repairs.
The work of it requires a sandbar
and wading waist deep. Anchors
and halyards. Mechanical advantage
of block and line. The work requires
many kinds of strength combined
with various subtle pressures.

—

Tides erode days until
there is only one: we drive,

we swim; waves break and
gather. I keep telling

the story; I worry there's
nothing more to know.

Again, I circle back; this is
the rind of the orange, the pit

of the peach; also the sweet,
also the tender. Also the tooth.

Author

Nancy Kuhl's recent books include *Granite* (A Published Event 2021), *The Birds of the Year* (Grenfell Press 2017), and *Pine to Sound* (Shearsman 2015). She is Curator of Poetry for the Yale Collection of American Literature, Beinecke Rare Book and Manuscript Library, Yale University, and a founding editor of Phylum Press. www.phylumpress.com.

On the cover

Women of the Peralta family, hand painted ambrotype; possibly by William Shew, circa 1855. Beinecke Rare Book and Manuscript Library, Yale University.

CPSIA information can be obtained
at www.ICGtesting.com
Printed in the USA
LVHW040341140722
723387LV00002B/331